when I was a
flower girl

Designer Fiona Walker

Commissioning Editor Annabel Morgan

Production Patricia Harrington

Picture and Location Manager Kate Brunt

Art Director Gabriella Le Grazie

Publishing Director Alison Starling

First published in the United States in 2002
by Ryland Peters & Small, Inc
519 Broadway
5th Floor
New York, NY 10012
www.rylandpeters.com

10 9 8 7 6 5 4 3 2 1

ISBN 1 84172 315 0

Printed and bound in China.

Front cover photography: Craig Fordham; back cover
photography, from left to right: Craig Fordham,
Polly Wreford, Caroline Arber; spine Polly Wreford.

when I was a flower girl

Antonia Swinson

RYLAND
PETERS
& SMALL

LONDON NEW YORK

when I was a flower girl

This book belongs to ✏ ....

I live at ....

and am .... years old. I was a flower girl at the

wedding of .... and ...., which took place

at ....and afterward at ....

.... on .... at ....

I know the bride and groom because ....

....

using this book

By filling in this book, you'll create a lovely record of your day as a flower girl that you'll find fun to read in years to come. Write down as many details as you can before the wedding and complete the rest soon afterward—it's surprising how quickly you can forget small details. Ask your mom or dad if they will take photographs on the day of the things you want to include. You might want to keep your wedding invitation and your place card from the reception, and you could also press or dry some of the flowers from your bouquet.

place
photo
here

a photo of the bride and groom

Congratulations

being a flower girl

It's a great honor to be asked to be a flower girl. It shows how much the bride and groom like you and how well they think you'll carry out this important role. As a flower girl you're a member of the bridal party. Your main job is to help the bride, and in this you will be joined by bridesmaids or other flower girls and ring bearers (together you're known as the "attendants"). You'll travel to the wedding ceremony with some of the other attendants and arrive just before the bride. When the bride arrives, she is likely to need help with her dress or veil, and she may ask her bridesmaids, or you, to assist her. Then get ready to walk down the aisle, scattering flower petals as you go, while the bride follows you into the ceremony to meet the groom.

who's who at the wedding

The bride and groom
The stars of the day! Give them both a kiss after the ceremony and say
a big thank-you for asking you to be their flower girl.

The maid or matron of honor
The maid of honor (she's called a matron if she's married) is a relative
or close friend of the bride and is her main helper on the day. She
stands with the bride and holds her bouquet during the ceremony.
She will tell you what to do if you're not quite sure.

The best man
He is a relative or close friend of the groom and is there to help him.
The best man looks after the wedding rings before the ceremony and
stands with the groom during it. He may make a toast at the reception.

The bride's father
He walks down the aisle with his daughter. (Sometimes the bride is
given away by another male relative or a friend.)

the other attendants

A bride often has a number of different attendants in her bridal party. There will probably be several bridesmaids, who are usually sisters, cousins, or close friends of the bride and groom. There may be some other flower girls too, who'll be a similar age to you, and perhaps there will be a ring bearer, who will also be about your age.

The bride and groom may ask some of their friends and relatives to act as groomsmen or ushers at the wedding ceremony. They will help by greeting the guests as they arrive and handing them ceremony programs before showing them to their seats.

Preparations

my outfit

As a flower girl, you will wear a beautiful outfit chosen for you by the bride to go with her dress. Bridesmaids and flower girls usually wear a special dress in a gorgeous fabric. The bride usually wears white or cream, but her attendants often wear a different color.

Whatever the bride chooses, she will probably ask you what you enjoy wearing so she can be sure you'll like it. You might go on an outing to buy your clothes from a store. If a dressmaker makes them, she'll need to measure you to make sure your dress fits perfectly. It's very exciting when you see your outfit for the first time, and once it's ready, you're bound to want to try it on. Just make sure you don't get it creased or dirty!

What my outfit was like

✏️

....

....

....

....

....

Where it was bought or who made it

....

....

When I went to buy it or try it on

....

....

....

....

....

my hair and accessories

Pretty accessories will add the finishing touch to your outfit. If you get new shoes for the wedding, it's important that they're comfortable, so say if they aren't. Practice wearing them at home so you can get used to them and ask your mom to rub the soles with sandpaper so you don't slip over. Flower girls often wear a headdress. This might be a circlet of flowers, a tiara, a decorated hairband, or pretty barrettes or combs. Your hair will be arranged specially, either by a hairdresser or your mom. They'll also pin your headdress in your hair. Try not to fiddle with it—you want your hair to look perfect!

What my shoes were like ....

....

What my headdress was like ....

....

Who arranged my hair ....

....

the bride's dress

The bride wears a very special outfit for her wedding. The traditional choice is a long dress in white or cream, although some brides wear short dresses or even pants, and some choose a different color. Wedding dresses can be made in all sorts of wonderful fabrics, such as lace, satin, velvet, tulle, or taffeta.

The bride usually keeps all the details of her outfit a big secret from everybody—especially the groom—until the morning of the wedding, so you'll have a lovely surprise when you arrive to get ready. Remember to tell her how beautiful she looks. If the bride's dress is very long and forms a train behind her, be extremely careful not to step on it!

What the bride's dress was like

What her veil, headdress, and shoes were like

place
photo
here

a photo of me in my dress

a drawing of me in my dress

the wedding rehearsal

Usually, there is a wedding rehearsal before the big day. Most brides and grooms feel a little bit nervous about the ceremony, so the rehearsal is a good opportunity for everyone to find out exactly what happens when and what they have to do. The best man, the bride's parents, and the groom's parents attend the rehearsal, along with the bride and groom. The attendants also go along so that you're all familiar with the venue for the ceremony and can be shown where you'll walk and stand on the wedding day. If you can't go, don't worry—you'll be told exactly what to do on the day by the maid of honor or another grown-up.

When the rehearsal was held ....

....

....

....

....

....

....

Who was there ....

....

....

....

....

....

The big day

getting ready

The wedding day has finally arrived! You're bound to be feeling very excited and perhaps a little nervous, so take a few deep breaths to calm yourself.

Eat a big breakfast so you won't get hungry later and have a bath. Perhaps your mom will let you add bubble bath so you smell delicious and are squeaky clean!

You'll probably get ready with the bride and all the other attendants, and your mom or a bridesmaid will help you get dressed. Resist the temptation to put on your wedding clothes too early—you don't want them to get dirty or crumpled. Once you arrive at the wedding venue, smile and make the most of every moment of this special day.

place
photo
here

a photo of me getting ready

the flowers

Beautiful flower arrangements are one of the things that make a wedding such a special occasion. The ceremony venue and reception are usually decorated with flowers—see how many you can spot and what they're like. Most brides carry flowers, which could be anything from a pretty posy to a big, spectacular bouquet. The groom, best man, and groomsmen usually wear flowers in their buttonholes. You'll probably be given flowers to carry—either a little bunch, or flowers in a basket or twined around a hoop. If you take them home after the wedding, you could try drying or pressing them as a keepsake.

What the flowers at the ceremony were like ....

....

What the flowers at the reception were like ....

....

What the bride's bouquet was like ....

....

What my flowers were like ....

....

the ceremony

At a religious ceremony in a church, the bride stands at the top of the aisle next to the groom, facing the minister. The minister conducts the service, during which there are usually hymns and readings. At the marriage itself, the bride and groom make special promises (vows) to love and support each other all their lives. When the ceremony is over, everyone processes back down the aisle and out of the church.

At a Jewish wedding in a synagogue, the bride and groom stand under a canopy called a chuppah to be married by the rabbi. At a civil ceremony, a justice of the peace takes the place of a minister. There may also be music and readings, though they probably won't be religious. You'll be expected to sit quietly during the wedding service, particularly the marriage vows themselves. Be patient—there will be lots of time to chat and have fun later.

photographs of the ceremony

the reception

The reception is the party that follows the wedding ceremony. Sometimes the bride and groom greet the guests in a receiving line, standing with their parents at the entrance to say hello to everyone as they enter.

At the reception, food is served—perhaps a sit-down meal or a buffet, or canapés on trays. Toasts may be made by the bride's father, the groom, and the best man. It's traditional for the groom to thank the attendants for doing such a good job!

The bride and groom will also cut their wedding cake. Once the first cut has been made, the cake is taken away and sliced up so everyone can try some.

Sometimes, there's dancing after the meal. The bride and groom's "going away" is at the end of the reception.

Who I sat with

Who I talked to

What we ate

Who made the toasts

What the cake was like

photographs of the reception

photographs of the reception

going away

All good things have to come to an end, and eventually it will be time for the bride and groom to leave for their honeymoon. It's traditional for everyone to gather together to say goodbye and wave them on their way. The bride and groom usually change out of their wedding clothes into special going-away outfits and will probably be driven away in a car. They'll then travel to their honeymoon destination.

*a photo of the
bride and groom*

What time the bride and groom left 🖉 ....

....

What they wore ....

....

Where they went on honeymoon ....

....

place
photo
here

my favorite photo of the day

happy memories

You're bound to be very tired after such an exciting and fun day and will need a good night's sleep. The day after a wedding can seem a little flat and boring, but there are lots of things you can be doing.

This is a good time to write a thank-you letter to the bride and groom if they gave you a present. You can also fill in all the remaining blanks in this book while everything's still fresh in your mind. Make sure you write down all the things you liked best. In years to come, you'll enjoy being able to re-live your special day as a flower girl.

What I liked best about being a flower girl

....

....

....

....

My favorite memory of the day

....

....

....

....

Photography credits

key: a = above, b = below, c = center, r = right, l = left

Caroline Arber: 3, 12 al, 12 br, 15 ar, 15 br, 16, 17 r of c, 18–19, 29 r, 35, 44;

Craig Fordham: 2, 4, 6, 8, 9 r, 10, 11, 14, 15 al, 17 l of c, 17 cr, 17r, 21, 28, 30, 33, 36–37, 40–41;

Polly Wreford: 1, 7, 9 l, 9 cl, 9 cr, 9 r of c, 17 l, 17 cl, 23, 24, 26–27, 29 l, 29 l of c, 29 cl, 29 r of c, 38–39, 42–43, 46, 48; Viv Yeo: 9 l of c, 12 ar, 12 bl, 15 bl, 29 cr.

Publisher's Acknowledgments

Ryland Peters & Small would like to thank David and Annabel, Justin and Lizzie, and Jamie and Berenice for graciously allowing us to photograph their weddings. Many thanks also to Jane Durbridge. Finally, a huge thank you to all our beautiful little flower girls.

Author's Acknowledgments

Thank you to David and Hannah for all their love and support, and to the helpful, efficient, and creative team at Ryland Peters & Small, in particular my editor, Annabel.